Tuning
Your Guitar

By Donald Brosnac.

Contents

New York/London/Sydney/Tokyo/Cologne

Exclusive distributors:
Music Sales Limited
78 Newman Street, London W1P 3LA, England.
Music Sales Pty. Limited
27 Clarendon Street, Artarmon, Sydney, NSW 2064, Australia.
Music Sales GmbH
Kölner Strasse 199, 5000 Cologne 90, West Germany.

This book © Copyright 1979 by
Guitar Workshop Publications
ISBN 0.86001.550.5
Order No. GW 10066

Foreword

From the most talented, professional musician to the beginner with his first guitar, there are times when tuning can be a frustating experience.

This book is written to help you tune your instrument as well as it can be done. The first two chapters are very basic, later chapters are more complex. Even if you are a skilled teacher, these first chapters may have a point or two you can use. I suggest that you read them when you can.

I often refer to nylon string guitars and metal string guitars. Please note that nylon string guitars use three bass strings that have a nylon core but a metal wrapping. These are referred to as nylon strings. By appearance, they might be confused with all-metal strings using a metal wire core, with a metal wrapping. Do not use all-metal strings on a nylon string guitar. It will injure the guitar. There are only two types of guitars that use nylon strings, classic guitars, which are quite common and Flamenco guitars.

The guitar has not always had six strings -- and been tuned E, A, D, G, B, E. Early guitars had four strings. Later that was amended so that some guitars had five strings, while others had eight strings (four double courses). Rival schools of music were at war and the victor was the five string guitar, with single courses, which received an extra string. The six string guitar! Some did add double courses to this instrument but 12 string classic guitars have never been popular.

Now we have mainly six string guitars with single courses. The tuning as mentioned earlier is E, A, D, G, B, E. The low E is referred to as string number 6 and the high E is number 1. A is 5, D is 4, G is 3, and B is 2.

When fretting strings your fingertips should be just behind the fret being fingered. On top of the fret, your fingers will deaden the sound. Too far back and the string will rattle because it is not securely against the fret.

FIGURE 1 All the notes on a guitar. Notes repeat after the twelfth fret.

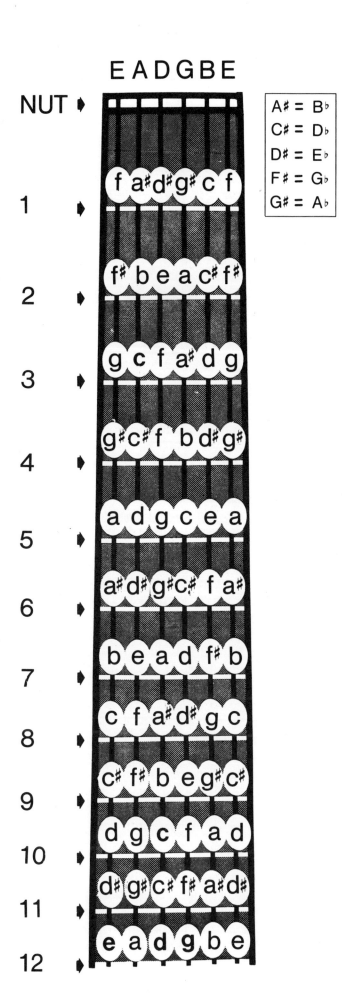

FIGURE 2 Parts of a guitar.

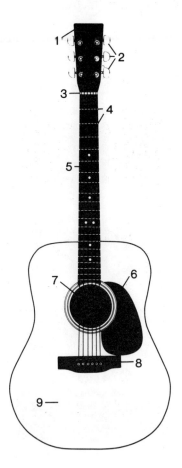

Shown is a front view of a steel string acoustic guitar. 1. Peghead. 2. Peghead is a term carried over from when all guitars had friction tuning pegs, like a violin. It holds the Tuning machines. Flamenco guitars still have them. 3. Nut. It forms the stopping point for one end of the string's open length. It also regulates spacing. 4. Frets. Traditionally, classic guitars have 18-19 frets, steel string guitars 20, and electrics 21 to 24. 5. Fretboard. This is the thin piece of wood the frets are inserted into. The neck is under the fretboard. It is also referred to as the arm. It runs from the peghead to where it ends, joining the body (box) of the guitar. The heel is the lower portion of the neck where it joins the body. 6. Pickguard. This is very rarely used on a classic guitar. 7. Soundhole. 8. Bridge. The bridge has a slanted insert on steel string guitars and a straight insert on classics. 9. Soundboard or top.

Whereas classic guitars traditionally don't have markings on the fretboard for the fifth, seventh, ninth and twelfth frets, virtually all metal strung guitars do. Electric guitars ordinarily have many frets marked. If you have a classic guitar with no markers and you get lost, you can have a guitar repairman inlay them. Normally they are dots of about 3/16 inch of Mother of Pearl on the fretboard top, and 1/16 inch ivory or plastic dots on the left edge of the fretboard. You could even glue on little circles you've punched out of paper and written the names on.

Your first instrument

O.K., you finally decided to buy that guitar you always wanted. How thrilled you were when you bought it at the music store where you looked at it so often. You got it home, careful not to get a scratch on it. You open your book "How to Play the Guitar." Achieving amazing contortions of your left hand you manage to finally position your finger tips on the strings as the diagram had shown. Now play your first notes on a guitar! Wait a minute!! That sounded terrible.

Something is wrong. You remember when you bought the guitar, the man at the store said: "Here, I'll tune it for you." You saw him turn six knobs at the long, skinny end of the guitar. Maybe you happened to hear the sound change when he turned the knobs, which are used to adjust the sound of the strings. Each string is connected to its own geared machine (called a tuning machine) which in turn has its own knob (called a button). The strings can be stretched tightly to make a high note or loosened to make a lower note. By using the tuning machines an instrument can be adjusted so each string is the proper note. You could return to the store and ask to have it retuned. That might be a little embarrassing, and what if when you got home it was not in proper tune again? You wonder what happened to the guitar. Why is it not in tune now? In the store it was.

Instruments with strings go out of tune very easily. The strings stretch (it's normal) and loosen. The weather causes different parts of the instrument to expand and contract, and so this can affect the tuning. You think, "Well, if that man at the store could tune it, then I should be able to." But you don't know what to do. That's what this book is for.

If you have never tuned a guitar before, it would be best to see how well your ear can discriminate notes. There are two tuning tools you can use for checking your hearing. First buy a little pitch pipe for the note E at a music store. A pitch pipe is a device that consists of a plastic tube with a thin strip of metal inside. When you blow into it, the metal strip vibrates and you hear the note it was designed to make. You can buy a combination of six pipes designed to make a note for each guitar string. They also make combination pipes for other instruments, as well as a radial pitch pipe with all the notes of an octave.

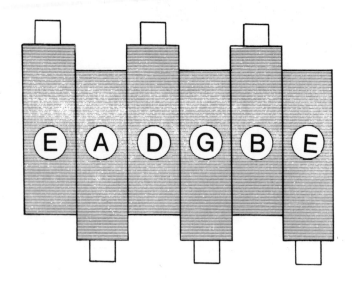

FIGURE 3 Pitch pipe. Combination of six for guitar.

Having bought your pitch pipe, ask the sales-person to play an E note on a guitar while you blow on the E pitch pipe. Ask the person to play the notes just above and below E. Listen closely. Does it sound pleasant to you when you both play E? Do the sounds blend together? Does it sound unpleasant, or do you hear waves of sound (beats) when you don't play exactly the same note? Have the person play E on several different strings. Hear how the sounds blend.

The second note-discrimination tuning tool is a tuning fork, which is more precise than a pitch pipe. It is both more expensive and awkward. As soon as you can, use a tuning fork for the note A. A tuning fork is very accurate and this is necessary if you ever play with someone else.

To use a tuning fork hold it near the bottom of the Y and tap the top of the Y against some hard rubber or similar material. Touch the bottom of the Y against the top of the guitar. Hear how the guitar has amplified the note. If you use a tuning fork with a solid body guitar you can either place the vibrating fork's ball end against the wood of the body or find a wooden cigar box. A wooden cigar box amplifies the sound nicely.

So now you can use a pitch pipe to sound A and use the tuning machine to tighten or loosen the A string until both are the same note -- or you can use a tuning fork. A tuning fork gives a purer sound than a pitch pipe. This can help in identi-fying pitches, and so assist discrimination in hearing. If you can do this, proceed to page 12. If you cannot hear whether two notes are the same or not, continue to page 8.

Developing perfect pitch

I feel we should refer to acute sensitivity and discrimination of pitch as absolute pitch, not perfect pitch. The latter relates to perfect pitches, i.e., notes, and this is easily confused with pure pitches and scales. Perfect also implies that there is no room for improvement, which suggests the condition has no beginning or end. My experiences suggest that "perfect pitch" may be acquired, that is, learned. Some children possess it at very young ages. This is undeniable. The possibility of someone being able to develop their once undiscriminating hearing to this state appears to be proved by many musicians.

Perfect pitch can be learned. Though some people appear to be born with it, most of us will have to cultivate it. If you use a tuning fork for a while, you start to become orientated to its exact pitch. You can almost hear it from memory. You won't realize this until one day when putting on new strings. Incredible! You nearly have it perfectly in tune already. How did this happen? Was it chance? No. You are training your ear. If you persist in this aural training, you should be able to match the fifths of the strings played open. Begin by tuning the A string to the memory you have. Now you play the A and the E. You adjust the E until it's a fifth lower and the pulsing beats blend into one harmonious chord. That is, almost blend together. You will be adjusting it to the tempered scale, right? You can give yourself a diploma now, for you have educated your ears. It is something you thought could never be done. But it can be done; it just takes a lot of practice.

In training the ear to distinguish pure unisons, the use of a double strung instrument such as a twelve-string guitar or a mandolin is helpful. Grasp one of the tuning buttons of the highest tuned pair of strings. Now turn the button very slowly. This will instantly produce an exceedingly unpleasant effect of regular pulsations or beats. Now turn the button back and listen attentively to the decreasing number of beats until the sounds merge into one continuous note. Octaves are somewhat akin to unisons in that when properly tuned there should be but one apparent sound, i.e., no beats. If each fifth were tuned "perfect", the final note of the guitar would be too sharp.

Your eyes can help your ears

If you don't have a developed ability to hear if a string is tuned correctly or not, let me explain a method I have developed. When I had my first guitar, I had such a hard time trying to tune it that twice I put it up for sale. I thought I would never learn to tune it.

My guitar sounded terrible when I played more than one string at once. My instruction book said to blow into a pitch pipe and use the tuning machines to adjust the pitch (note) of the strings to match. It said to tighten the string if its note was too low and to loosen the string if its note was too high. But how can you tell if it is too high or low if you can't hear the difference?

Notice that earlier I mentioned, "A developed sense of hearing." You can learn to hear better! Some people are gifted with superb hearing, but most people must practise to achieve sensitive hearing. The following exercise can help you on the road to better hearing. Many music teachers may dislike such a crutch; but if your hearing is as bad as mine was, you may have to start this way.

Can you hear with your eyes? Not really, but they can help your ears. The following technique could be used by the blind, although they would have to use their finger tips to detect the motion we will be trying to see.

The following method can often be used successfully, but generally a guitar must have been put in proper tune recently. If a guitar has not been tuned properly, it most likely will not be satisfactory. If you can use a pitch pipe to help you tune some of the strings, do so.

Pluck a string with a finger. See it move? Look *very* closely at it. See it vibrate back and forth? It moves so fast it becomes almost transparent. Now do this in the sunlight. Notice, you have to look *very* closely, because the strings that have a wrapping of wire glisten when they vibrate in the sunlight. Notice that the glistening strings have faint colours of the rainbow, which makes noticing vibrations easier.

If one string is plucked and another string is tightened so it is the same note, the plucked, vibrating string will cause the untouched string with the same note to vibrate. This effect is called a sympathetic vibration.

Place a finger on the string you've plucked,

push it against the fretboard, and then slide your finger up and down the string. Pluck the string whenever you move from one metal cross strip on the guitar's neck to another. These metal strips, called frets, are used to select different open vibrating lengths for the strings. Shorter lengths result in higher notes. The guitar will be in tune when the following string-to-string matching is accomplished.

A *reference note* is needed to begin tuning. This could be the note of any string, but it is helpful if the reference string is the A string. The A string should be tuned to A for this tuning method to be accurate. A guitar can be tuned *relative* to *any note*, either higher or lower than A, but it will not develop its best tone.

This is how a guitar which is in tune should behave. The following procedures can be used to achieve this.

Finger a string with one hand and pluck it with the other. Watch to see if any string moves when you are not touching it. You could delicately feel for this. Watch when you press down string number 6 at the fifth fret to see if string number 5 vibrates. If it does not, chances are that either string number 6 or 5 is not correct. Now pluck string number 5 fingered at the fifth fret. If the untouched string number 4 moves, it means chances are very good it is the same note. Pluck both strings together while your finger stays on the 5th string. If they sound the same, they are the same note. This will give us a starting point.

If no string matches, check to see if any strings match when they are fingered at the third, fourth, or sixth fret. If a string is fingered at the sixth fret and it vibrates the string to its right, it means either it is too low or the string on the right is too high.

Say that when the 5th string is fretted at the fifth fret and then plucked, it vibrates the untouched 4th string. Notice when you pluck these strings that the fretted 5th string sounds like the untouched, open, 4th string. In fact both together sound like one string.

Now say, when you play the 4th string at the fifth fret, it does not move the open 3rd string. When you play both together it does not sound pleasant. If you listen carefully you can hear a pulsing sound. This results from the overlapping patterns of the two notes. If both were the same note, they would be vibrating together and you would hear one steady sound. This pulsing is referred to as a beat or beats. It may take a while for you to notice this. You hear it most clearly when notes are very close.

Now, back to our 4th string at the fifth fret. If it doesn't match the open 3rd string when it is played at the fifth fret, but if played unfretted it does match the 5th string at the fifth fret, this means the 3rd string is incorrect. Play the 4th string at the sixth fret. Does it match the 3rd string open? No? Then try moving your finger to the fourth fret. Aha! It now vibrates the 3rd string open. This means the 3rd string is too low. Notice you moved your finger and so the vibrating length of the 4th string changed. You made the string longer and so it made a lower note. This lower note matched the 3rd string. This shows the 3rd string is too low. Tighten the string by slowly turning the tuning machine button until you get

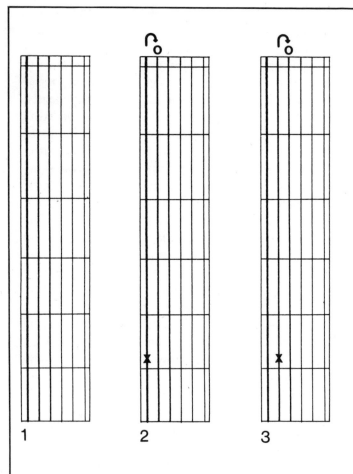

1   First the A string is tuned (or it is used as a point of reference without having its tuning checked).
An **o** in the diagram stands for a string played open— that is, unfretted.

2   The 6th string fretted at the fifth fret and plucked should vibrate the 5th string which is not touched.

3   The 5th string fretted at the fifth fret and plucked should vibrate the 4th string which is not touched.

the open 3rd string to match the 4th string fretted at the fifth fret. Proceed according to the chart diagrams given below.

A worthwhile matching variation is that of matching to one string. This minimizes progress sharping or flatting, common with fifth/fourth fret matching. See figure on page 16.

Another match is that of fretted descending octave matching, explained on page 17. This matching is meant more as an aid to checking tuning than as a method of tuning. These tuning methods are given in later chapters.

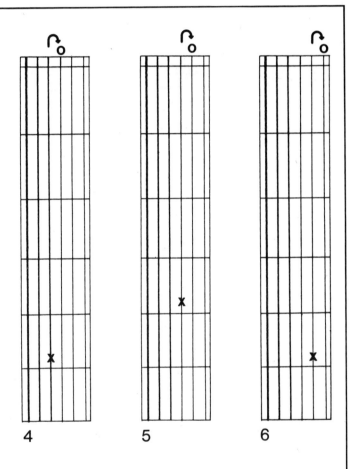

4   5   6

4   The 4th string fretted at the fifth fret and plucked should vibrate the 3rd string which is not touched.

5   The 3rd string fretted at the fourth fret and plucked should vibrate the 2nd string which is not touched.

6   The 2nd string fretted at the fifth fret and plucked should vibrate the 1st string which is not touched.

Basic tuning procedure

On page 8, I explained how to tune with the aid of the eye. Now we can do the same thing using education and ear power. For this we will have to learn a few of the notes shown in Figure 1.

Frets provide predetermined stopping points. These stopping points provide the varying string lengths that give us notes (which have been given alphabetical names).

Hmmm, this is getting complicated, isn't it? All those letter names for notes. But wait a minute. How come it goes A, B, C, D, E, F, G and then it starts all over again with A? This repeat is called an octave.

After comparing identical notes, the most basic note relationship is that of the octave. Octave means a particular relationship. By relationship it is meant the position of a note to another note.

It is sometimes confusing because we give the same name to notes in an octave relationship.

If we keep the size and tension on a string the same and shorten it by one-half, we get a note with the same name but higher in pitch--one octave higher. If the string is doubled in length, we also get an octave but now it is one octave lower. Since a vibrating string makes waves of motion, it is helpful to think of the size of waves to understand octaves and other musical relationships. A wave five inches long will be one octave higher than a wave ten inches long; a wave twenty inches will be one octave lower than a ten-inch wave, and two octaves lower than a five-inch wave.

It might be helpful to give an example of flashing lights to understand why notes of octaves are said to have similar sounds and so have the same name. Imagine one light flashing on and off ten times a second. Now add a light that flashes at exactly five times a second. The lights will continue flashing in step regardless of how long they are on. If one of the lights is made to flash at a slightly faster or slower rate they will no longer flash in an orderly rhythmic pattern.

The orderly rhythm of an octave relationship ----2 to 1---- is the building block of music and the most useful tool for tuning instruments. It is easy to tune using notes of the same wave length or octave differences, because it is easy to tell when they are out of step.

Measure the length of your guitar strings. Place your finger tip just behind the fret at one-half its length. Pluck the string. Then pluck the open string. These notes both have the same name. The distance between them is an octave. Any time you go from one note to the next closest note of the same value, you go an octave. Notice that the octave for an individual string is at the twelfth fret. On guitars, banjos, mandolins and all other classical, Western civilization fretted instruments, the twelfth fret is one octave higher than the open string. You can also make an octave from the second fret to the fourteenth fret, and so forth.

You have noticed that even though we only have the notes A, B, C, D, E, F, and G, we have more stopping places. Musicians use in-between spaces so music can be played in all keys (more on that a little later) and blend more gently. These spaces are called sharps or flats, depending on whether you are going up or down the scale. The signs for these are ♯ for sharp and ♭ for flat. We then have A (A♯B♭), B, C (C♯D♭), D (D♯E♭), E, F (F♯G♭) G (G♯A♭). Because of the way our ears work, there are no half steps between B and C and E and F. The reason for this is a bit complicated, but it is not important for us right now.

For our interest now, all we need know is that the half step spaces are the distances between frets. Count all the notes—full notes and half notes and half steps. See that there are twelve of them. That is why the octave is at the twelfth fret. Now Figure 1 with the names of all the notes can make sense, even if it's still a bit frightening. You don't have to know very many notes to tune your guitar. In fact, all you *must* know is one. Through that one you'll find out what the other five are for the remaining five strings.

If we know that one of the E strings is correct, we can go from one string to the next and so tune all the strings. We do this by finding the note we need for the next string to be tuned on the string we just tuned.

Now when we match we should know what the name of the note is. Why do we need to know that? Well, because your instrument was made to be used with strings just so tight. If they are too

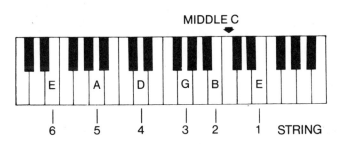

FIGURE 4 Tuning a guitar from a piano — where to find the correct notes.

tight they will break; if they are too loose they will not have a full sound. If two guitar players have their guitars in proper tune, then they will be in tune *together*. They then can play together and make pleasant music.

How can we tune to the proper notes? We need something that will make a proper note. If we had a properly tuned piano we could just press, say, an E and then tune the E string. Then press an A key and tune the guitar's A string and so forth. But what if we don't have a properly tuned piano handy? We can use a pitch pipe. The pitch it gives is marked on its outside. We can buy one and then match notes from string to string, or we can buy a combination pitch pipe with six pitches (notes). Pitch pipes are cheap, and because they are cheap they don't always work right. What does always work right is a tuning fork. You can buy tuning forks in different notes. Because of the way a scale is arranged, I suggest you buy an A tuning fork.

To use a tuning fork, hold it by the ball end, strike it against something that will cause it to

FIGURE 5 Tuning fork for A-440 cycles per second.

vibrate but not harm it, then place the ball end against the bridge or top of the guitar. The guitar will increase the sound. Adjust the A string until it blends with the sound of the tuning fork. You may have to hit it again. Then you can match strings across. To buy six tuning forks would be expensive and bulky, and there are more efficient methods.

Now finger the 6th string at the fifth fret and pluck it. Does it match the sound of the plucked open A string? Adjust the machine of the 6th string until it does.

Now finger the 5th string, the A string, at the fifth fret and pluck. This is the note D. The 4th string needs to be tuned to D. Does the plucked open 4th string match it? Adjust the 4th string until it does.

Finger the 4th string at the fifth fret and pluck. This gives us G. The 3rd string needs to be tuned to G. Pluck the open 3rd string and adjust it to match the fingered 4th string.

Finger the 3rd string at the fourth fret and pluck. This will give us the note B. Pluck the open 2nd string and adjust until it is B also.

Finger the 2nd string at the fifth fret and pluck. This will give us E. Pluck the open 1st string and adjust it until it also is E.

Now check to see if strings 1 and 6 sound like the same note, E, but are two octaves apart. They should be.

Tuning to one string

If you find that the two E strings do not

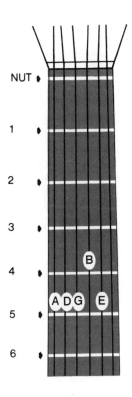

FIGURE 6 Traditional tuning method. Matching across the 5/4 frets.

match when you use the above procedure, you may find the following a solution to your problems.

First tune the A string, preferably by using a tuning fork. Now fret the 6th string at the fifth fret and pluck. It should be A; adjust it so it is. No beats should be heard with the matching of identical notes, even if they are octaves apart.

Now fret the 4th string at the seventh fret. This should be A; adjust so it is.

Fret the 3rd string at the second fret. This should be A. Fret the 2nd string at the tenth fret. This should be A. Fret the 1st string at the fifth fret. This should be A.

Note that A is accurately tuned with a pitch device and all other strings are tuned relative to it. This eliminates progressive sharpening or flatting when tuning from one string to another, and then to another. This, along with octave harmonics, is the most accurate method of tuning fretted stringed instruments. The performing and use of harmonics is given in the next chapter.

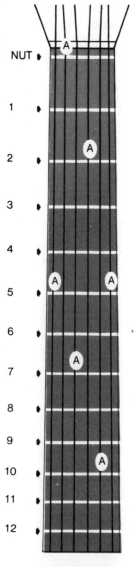

FIGURE 7 Tuning all strings to the A string which is tuned to a tuning fork. Notice where A is found on all the strings, so it can be matched to the open A string.

Varied matching patterns

There are many matching patterns for tuning. Sometimes you'll use several of them when you have to tune a difficult instrument such as a twelve-string guitar.

Shown earlier was the matching at the fifth and fourth fret. Some people prefer to match, say, an open 6th string with the 5th string played at the seventh fret. You can see from the earlier chart that this is an octave range.

How to finger harmonics

Tuning by harmonics can be done, but it must be done using octaves or it will not be accurate. Using only fifth and seventh fret harmonics will result in pure intervals, not tempered tuning. A guitar cannot be tuned accurately using this method.

Assuming that A is tuned, place a finger tip of the left hand very lightly on the A string above the twelfth fret. Do not press the string down to the fret. Touch very lightly. With the right hand pluck the string. Then pluck it again and remove the lefthand finger tip as soon as the string is plucked. Try this on other strings at the twelfth fret. The sound you hear is that of the strings, halves vibrating together. It is the octave (twelfth fret, remember?) harmonic. It is such a pure tone that it is easy to hear it precisely. Now place your finger on the D string above the seventh fret. Play the harmonic there. This is the note of A on the D string. This is the tone to be matched with A's octave harmonic. Notice that your hand is free to adjust the tuning machines with this method. The only problem is that when you come to the octave harmonic of the G string you will have to fret the B string at the eighth fret for an audible matching note. Use the charts to figure out what the rest of the harmonic matches are. The remaining ones are all at the twelfth and seventh frets.

Fretted octave matches

By using sliding fretted octave matches, greater accuracy in tuning may be obtained. This may also indicate that difficult tuning is caused by your guitar, not your ears.

Finger C by placing your index finger on the B string (2nd string) at the first fret. Now finger C on the A string (5th string) by placing your ring finger on that string at the third fret. The notes are the same but an octave apart.

Now put your index finger on the 1st string, first fret. This is F. If you place your ring finger on the 4th string, third fret, you will have fingered F, an octave lower. These notes should blend. You can slide these formations up and down the fretboard, and if the spacing (in frets) between them is kept constant they should remain in tune with each other. Look for other possible matches. Find out how the 1st and 6th strings could perform sliding matches. Find out how the 1st and 3rd strings can be matched. See Figure 8.

Slide these matched octaves up and down the fretboard. Try to adjust the tuning machines so that all positions stay equally in tune when you move them. If your guitar cannot be equally in tune in a multitude of these positions, there must be something wrong with either the guitar or your strings. Make sure you aren't bending some of the strings and so raising their pitch.

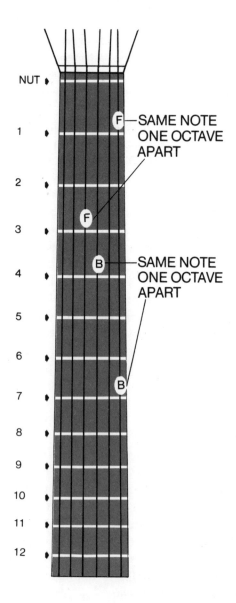

FIGURE 8 Finding octaves on a guitar to check whether all notes are equally in tune.

Problems caused by instruments

Hopefully your ear is becoming a bit more discriminating. If your ear is sensitive and your instrument is not tuneable, then your *instrument* is incorrect. Before we take out our hostility on our guitars, let's see what we can do to help.

Unless you have a "made-in-my-garage special", the frets are probably in the right place. It is very, very rare to find incorrectly spaced frets on commercial guitars. So rare that it doesn't warrant much discussion.

Tuning machines

Assuming your guitar's neck or body isn't broken, the number one enemy of tuning is a defective tuning machine. It must have precise action. The gears must mesh perfectly. A sloppy fit means a sloppy tuning. Unfortunately, even top quality machines are sometimes defective. Machines can feel fairly tight but still slip minutely, causing intense fury because the player doesn't know what's wrong.

Though all guitars with vertical machines and solid pegheads are suited to metal strings, some guitars with horizontal machines and slotted pegheads are also suited for metal strings. How can you tell? Look at the rollers in the peghead slots which the strings wrap around. Are they about three-eighths inch diameter and white? Then they are either plastic, bone or ivory and are only suited for nylon strings. If they are about three-sixteenths inch in diameter and metal, then at least silk-and-steel, if not all-metal strings should be used. It is best to check with a music store though, since cheap guitars with metal rollers cannot take the stress of anything but nylon. Most times the combination of metal rollers and a pin bridge means that metal strings are O.K.

The wide rollers are used on a nylon-string guitar in order to provide a greater rate of change with each revolution than a small diameter roller would provide. Since metal strings are much more sensitive to tension changes because they are less elastic, they use small-diameter rollers.

Flamenco guitars should have wooden friction pegs similar to those on a violin, for the same reason that violins do not have geared metal tuning machines. Place a vibrating tuning fork on a metal machine and then on a wooden peg. If you can't tell the difference, you had better take up tambourine. Metal is dead. Wood sings. Wooden pegs are harder to adjust than geared machines and are not so strong. Since a flamenco guitar is built to be loud and bright with short duration of plucked tones, wooden pegs are complementary. Flamenco guitars always use nylon strings.

Violin shops sell a soft, waxy peg lubricant for smooth turning. If pegs are too slippery, they can be treated with talc. If these materials are used by the owner and do not suffice, leave the problems to an experienced violin repairman. Few guitar repairmen are competent with friction pegs.

Because of their heavy weight, which aids sustain (the duration of tone), the metal enclosed-gear, metal-button, Grover, or Schaller tuning machines are best adapted to solid-body electric guitars. Their heaviness often upsets the balance of an acoustic guitar, making the peghead a chore to hold up. This is a definite problem with twelve-string guitars. Many acoustic guitars have these machines because they are of a high quality. These machines are sealed with lubricant inside. The only adjustment point is the screw on the end of the button -- tighten the screw and the turning action is tighter.

Another model of machine is the open-gear style. The only adjustment here is the screw that holds the worm gear to the shaft. This periodically comes loose and needs to be tightened so the action is not loose and inaccurate. The best lubricant for open-back machines is a dry graphite lube. Oil collects dust which wears down the gears.

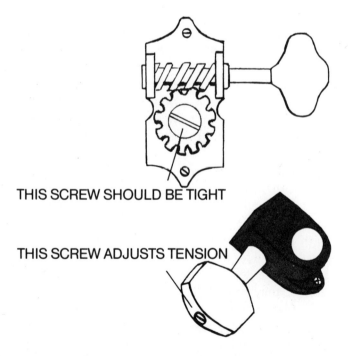

THIS SCREW SHOULD BE TIGHT

THIS SCREW ADJUSTS TENSION

FIGURE 9 Tuning machines, open back and enclosed models.

Machines should be securely held to the peg-head with small screws, as looseness makes tuning difficult. Sometimes there are tabs which do not hold the button shaft gear securely. Often it is possible to remove the machine and lightly hammer down the tabs to reduce the free play.

Problems of scale length, nut and frets

The placement of the frets on a fretboard is almost always quite accurate. Though most in-accuracies occur with the placement of the bridge, the placement of the nut can also be troublesome. Some guitar builders trim the edge of the fret-board that touches the nut so there is a good fit. Unfortunately, they have to trim it because they made a sloppy cut. When this is trimmed, the distance between the first fret and the nut is too short. The strings will then be out of tune. This is hard to detect. Measurement comparisons with other guitars using the same scale are useful here.

Just where the strings are stopped by the nut can be another problem. They need to be stopped at the edge of the nut that meets the end of the fretboard. If the notch in the nut is humped, the string will be stopped at a point in the middle of the nut.

A valid solution to the nut placement problem is the zero fret. The wood of the fretboard continues past where the nut would be located, at the precise stopping point of the strings, a notch is cut and a fret is inserted. Since the first fingerable fret is called the first fret, this is called a zero fret. A nut-like object is then positioned at the top of the fretboard to provide string spacing. Since the scale length and height is determined by the zero fret, the psuedo-nut is only a spacer, not a height regulator or stopping point. Unfortunately, the zero fret is most often used only on cheap guitars. There is no reason why it should not be used more often.

Problems with scale length, the bridge

The word intonation is derived from *intone*, which means to create a sound. By common usage *intonation* has come to mean the ability of a guitar to sound precisely the note values called for. For perfect *intonation* the nut, frets, and bridge must be in their proper places.

No guitar can play in tune unless the strings have the proper compensation length. All guitars, except those strung with nylon strings, can benefit from individually compensated bridge stopping points.

String compensation is the lengthening of the distance of the bridge from the nut, beyond that of the mathematically figured stopping point.

Say you have a classic guitar with a 26-inch

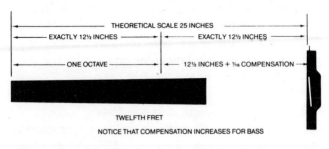

THEORETICAL SCALE 25 INCHES
EXACTLY 12½ INCHES
EXACTLY 12½ INCHES
ONE OCTAVE
12½ INCHES + 1/16 COMPENSATION
TWELFTH FRET
NOTICE THAT COMPENSATION INCREASES FOR BASS

FIGURE 10 What string compensation is.

scale. The frets are computed for the 26-inch distance. So, do we have the bridge stop the strings at exactly 26 inches? No. We add a little more distance and put the bridge there. This is because when we finger strings, the farther we go toward the bridge, the farther they are stretched in order to touch a fret. This extension of the length of a string is called string compensation. Setting of compensation is often referred to as setting intonation.

You can tell if the bridge is in the right place by playing the 12-fret harmonic on a string and then fretting the string at the twelfth fret and plucking it. Do the notes match? Are they exactly the same but one octave apart? If they are not and your strings and fretboard are correct, your guitar's bridge is in the wrong place.

Nylon-string guitars are made so that all the strings can use a common length. But even here the placement of the bridge's stopping point of the strings is two times the distance of the nut to the twelfth fret *plus* 1/32 to 1/16 of an inch. The determining factors are string size, tension, and action height.

Notice that the bridge insert, the ivory (or plastic on steel string guitars), is slanted. This is an attempt at providing the varying lengths needed.

For metal string guitars the string length should be: twice the distance from the nut to the twelfth fret plus 1/32-inch for a light gauge high E string. The heavier gauge strings need longer distances. Electric basses often have an inch of difference between E and G.

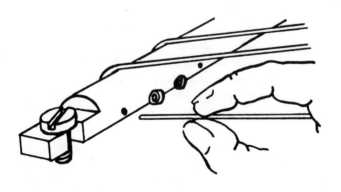

FIGURE 11 The old SG/Les Paul type bridge.

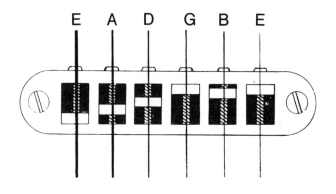

FIGURE 12 Adjustable bridge with basic arrangement for use with a wound G string.

Early Gibson SG guitars, as well as other Gibson guitars, had solid nonadjustable bridges. (In referring to nonadjustable vs. adjustable, I am talking about adjustability of bridge inserts for scale length. Many bridges are called adjustable but only their height is changeable.) These were made when Gibson Sonomatic strings with a wound G were the norm. These bridges which have a cast-in zig-zag pattern on top will be often quite accurate with the before-mentioned strings. Using an unwound G will make the guitar untuneable. The Gibson solid bridge with a smooth, unpatterned top will not be well in tune with any string. Gibson saw the light and no longer makes it. You can replace either of the before-mentioned bridges with a fully adjustable Leo Quan "Bad Ass Bridge." Another Gibson guitar that could benefit from more adjustable bridge settings is the Les Paul. However, often all that is necessary is to remove the screw from a bridge insert, turn the insert around, and replace the screw. The angled insert can then produce a range fully the width of the bridge insert channel.

There are many Gibson adjustable bridges that have plastic inserts. These produce a more mellow sound than metal bridge inserts, though some people want more bite in their sound and replace them with metal.

ADJUSTMENT SCREW FOR INTONATION

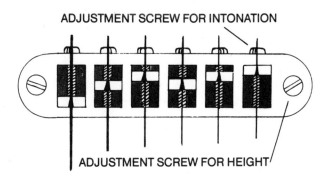

ADJUSTMENT SCREW FOR HEIGHT

FIGURE 13 Adjustable bridge for electric guitar. Basic insert arrangement for extra-light strings with a plain G string.

Most Fender guitars have satisfactory bridges. However, the Telecaster Standard is hard to tune because the intonation is only adjustable for two strings at a time. Yet no two strings should have the same location. Fortunately, Fender does sell a six-way Tele-bridge. All Teles should have them. Most other Fender guitars which have three insert bridges can be modified with Tele Six insert bridge pieces.

Most acoustic guitars are not played much past the twelfth fret. A simple slanted bridge saddle offers all the needed compensation. If there is playing over an extensive area of the fretboard, a compensation of individual strings is necessary. An adjustable bridge would be too heavy on an acoustic guitar. It's o.k. on an electric (weight helps sustain). A competent repairman can set up an acoustic guitar with individual ivory bridge pieces. It will then be necessary to stick to one gauge of string to be in tune. This is a fairly expensive job. Gretsch makes a three-piece bridge that other makers should adapt. It's superior to a single slant. The Martin guitars are so excellent in regard to tone and playability, it's odd why models such as the £1,000 plus D-45 don't have some form of compensation.

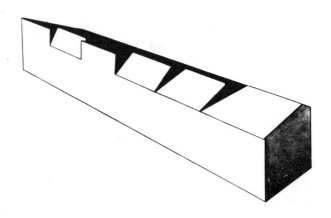

FIGURE 14   Bridge insert filed to provide string compensation.

Vibrato problems

All guitars with Vibrola-Vibrato Tremolo tailpieces suffer from tuning problems. Tuning problems are caused any time a device is added to a guitar that changes the pitch. In theory the strings should be returned to pitch after use, but in reality the loosening and stretching have side effects. Bigsby units are the least susceptible to tuning problems. The new Bigsby-made *Palm Pedal* is the most successful.

A mysterious tuning problem is that of a flexing unused vibrato. A guitarist says, "Why does it go out of tune?" He says he never uses the vibrato. What's to blame? When he bends notes, the added tension loosens all the other strings by pulling the vibrato unit forward. Result: out of tune. Solution: remove and replace the vibrato unit if it is not used with a non-vibrato unit.

Miscellaneous reasons why the guitar is hard to tune

Check these common structural defects: Loose parts flexing and so throwing the guitar out of tune? Are the neck and body breaking apart?

Is the bridge coming off? It needs to be pointed out here that many guitars have a removeable bridge. These bridges, most often on F hole guitars, will fall off completely when the strings are removed. The bridge should be positioned according to the before-mentioned information furnished concerning "bridges and intonation."

FIGURE 15 Bridge for F-hole guitar. Bridge is not glued in position and may be moved.

Is the top of the back loose from the sides?
Are the tuning machines securely fastened?
Are the strings securely fastened?
Is the nut broken loose and angling back towards the peghead?

Do you have a guitar strap tied to either end of the guitar, causing the neck to flex? If so, untie the strap from the peghead and install a strap button on the heel of the neck to hold the strap.

Is the peghead splintered?

Is the guitar so badly warped or worn that the strings hit the wrong fret when fingered or completely miss the saddle insert in the bridge?

Is the string stopped at the fret you finger? See if a string fingered at the fifth fret stops on the sixth fret. This will happen if one fret is too low and the next fret is too high. You will not then be able to tune the guitar. Likewise, if the bridge is rocking forward so the string goes completely over the insert without touching it, tuning it will be impossible. Both of these situations require corrections made by qualified guitar repairmen.

Is an unused capo left on a guitar, but slid above the nut? It is pressing the strings down. If it is moved down the neck into use position, the guitar will be out of tune. The pressure behind the nut has been removed.

Strings

The frequency of the fundamental note produced by a string depends on its tension, length, diameter and density. Increasing the length and/or decreasing the diameter will lower the note while the opposite will raise it.

A string vibrates in many patterns: the whole length, half-lengths, quarter lengths, one-third lengths, etc. The full length is the fundamental, the others are harmonic overtones. Since a string is vibrating in many ways, it is possible, especially in the case of worn strings, for a string to be out of tune with itself!

The complex vibrating patterns of a string demonstrate why attention to metallurgy, machining and heat treating is of such vast importance. If a string is not of precise uniform diameter it will cause erratic harmonics. Twisting, which adds stresses, is also to be avoided. In this light it is interesting that some string manufacturers are packaging strings straight in tubes instead of coiled. Violin strings have come packaged straight for years. Coiling cannot help strings in any way.

If you were to watch closely the pattern traces a plucked string makes on an oscilloscope,

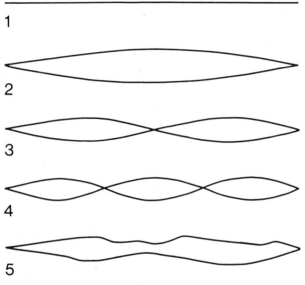

FIGURE 16 Vibrating patterns of strings. 1. string at rest 2. string vibrating in fundamental 3. string vibrating in octave harmonic 4. string vibrating in thirds 5. a typical, changing multiple pattern. (actual strings vibrate in many ways.)

you would see the variations that occur. Almost instantaneously after a string is plucked, the pitch raises from zero to slightly over its tuned pitch, and then it settles to that tuned pitch. After this the string, if it's in good condition, slowly goes flat. The string is quite noticeably flat when it is coming to rest and is barely audible. Strings in poor condition, such as old ones, go flat much sooner. In fact, they barely can remain at a desired pitch for even a moment.

Flexibility of the string's winding material affects the harmonic structure. Flat wound strings are easy to finger but are much less brilliant than round wound strings.

Yes, some strings are tuneable and others are not. Old worn strings affect tuning in three ways: 1. Strings become deformed by frets and this lumpy configuration is amazingly effective in throwing harmonics off. Broken or worn windings also produce this effect. 2. A buildup of sweat, dirt, corrosion and rust inhibit the strings' vibrations. This reduces the volume of the fundamentals and harmonics. 3. Strings lose their elasticity. They stop behaving like energy-filled springs and take on the character of a dead trout. Hit them and they go thud. This is the result of metal fatigue. Bronze strings lose their springiness quicker than nickel-steel strings. More research into metallurgy is definitely needed.

But how long do strings last? A generally agreed on time is about forty playing hours. I have found that strings may start to sound dead before forty hours, but won't cause serious tuning problems until about seventy-five hours time. This does depend on how much you sweat and how hard you play. If strings sit for too long, they can lose their springiness, i.e., sound dead. Don't buy strings in old dusty boxes.

Even the minute surface texture of the material of strings has an effect. Uneven textures produce uneven higher overtones. An even coarse texture can excite minute vibration patterns in the air and sound brighter. Smooth strings are the opposite. Since surface roughness is smoothed by playing and fretting, there are too many possible disadvantages to warrant the use of rough-surface-texture strings by those not possessing extensive string knowledge.

The strings' height above the fretboard and the diameter of them affect tuning. An electric guitar with extremely light strings and a string height of 3/32 of an inch over the twenty-fourth fret needs little bridge compensation. The high E can be stopped at exactly twice the distance of the nut to the twelfth fret. The remaining strings are positioned back from that. The higher the strings are or the larger gauges you use, the farther back the bridge must be.

If the strings are excessively high above the fretboard, a guitar can be totally untuneable. When fingering such strings, so much pressure must be applied that the fretted notes are too sharp. Strings are excessively high when they are more than 1/4 of an inch above the last fret. Some nylon string guitars are playable with 1/4 of an inch space. Low action on an electric guitar is a space of 3/32 of an inch. Acoustic steel string guitars need a little more space than electric guitars, since they are played more vigorously.

The stopping point is related to the stiffness of the string. With metal strings this is closely correlated to the central support wire. A plain G is fairly thick and so requires more compensation than a wound G which has a skinny support wire. The central wire diameter, not the wrapping diameter, is important.

Nylon-string guitars are made with straight bridges and use strings that are specifically made to have the same stopping point. The problem of string stretch is particularly a nylon-string problem. Metal strings stretch for about a day, but nylon strings often keep on stretching for almost a week. This is unavoidable. A nylon guitar should be able to hold tune for at least an hour's playing time after they have stretched for a day.

Especially important to nylon-string guitars is the proper fastening of the string ends. Traditionally nylon strings were tied at the bridge.

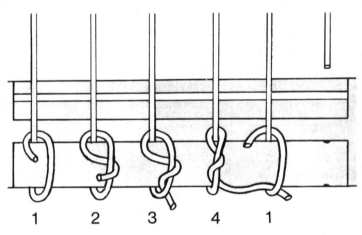

1   2   3   4   1

FIGURE 17 How to tie nylon strings onto a classic guitar bridge.

Though most strings for classic guitars tie onto the bridge, some other North European and American classics have pin bridges and use ball end strings. Nylon strings are made with ball ends for pin bridges, but their quality is never of the premium grade. Ball end strings can be used on *tie bridges* if you can't tie plain end strings. Just as important is the securing of the string in the tuning machine post. The routing of a string through a hole, back around the post, and then folding on itself is a secure fastening method.

Nylon strings often come in a package with strings E, A and D made of nylon filaments wound with either silver, gold alloy, or copper wire windings and silver plating. Strings G, B and E are often nylon mono filaments and may be clear or coloured. Some sets are made with nylon on nylon wound G and B strings. This adds brightness of tone if so desired.

Classic guitar strings are commonly available in low, medium, high, or very high tensions. Higher tension strings are often used for concerts since they are louder. They also have a bit more bright-

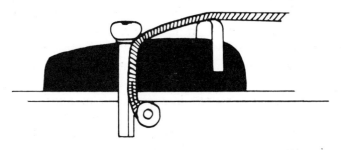

FIGURE 18 How strings attach using a pin bridge.

ness. Lastly, they are often quite expensive.

Some machines for metal strings have a notch and hole for fastening. For these, the end of the string is inserted in the deep hole. Then the string is bent sidewise and wrapped around the post.

Electric guitars either have the string's ball (or ring) end fastened by being threaded through: 1. the guitar body; 2. the bridge; 3. a tailpiece. F-hole guitars generally use a tailpiece.

Do not ever put metal strings on a guitar meant for nylon strings. These guitars cannot take such stress.

If you have an electric guitar with a magnetic pick-up, it is important to use strings that contain nickel. Guitars with piezo-electric pick-ups can use any type string. Your guitar has magnetic pick-ups if there are rectangular boxes under the strings that can attract an iron nail. Piezo pick-ups are most often mounted internally in guitar bridges.

If you use strings with bronze/copper windings on a magnetic/electric guitar, you will not get a clear sound and tuning will be impaired. Magnetic pick-ups are most responsive to nickel-wound strings.

For ultimate clarity of tone on an electric guitar, the strings should be as close to the pick-ups as possible. This distance is how close they can be without hitting the pick-ups or being pulled against the magnets. The closer the distance, the more the higher overtones will be sensed and the higher the volume will be. Most pick-ups have a height adjustment screw on either side of the pick-up. Some pick-ups have three screws so the angle of the top of the pick-up can be adjusted to conform to the angle of the strings. Many pick-ups, such as most

Gibson's, have screw adjustments under each string. These can be screwed up or down and control the pick-up's sensitivity to each string. These adjustable sensors are called pole pieces since they regulate the influence of the magnet's poles.

A defective tone control on an electric guitar or bass causes tuning difficulties because of its scratchy sound. This is the result of dirt inside the controls (potentiometers). An electronics repairman can clean them for a reasonable amount.

Acoustic steel string guitars use bronze-wrapped steel strings for the four lowest pitch strings. The bronze's softness actually translates into softer sound in comparison to an electric guitar's hard nickel wrapping. Bronze-copper alloys aid the formation of lower harmonics giving a fuller sound to acoustic guitars.

Cleaning strings in such fluids as petrol can extend their life if they do not suffer from wear. I have had quite good results recently from soaking strings in a concentrated solution of laundry enzyme pre-soak and water.

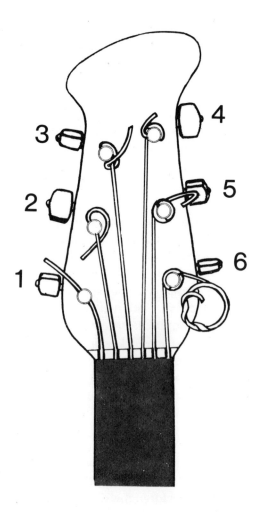

FIGURE 19 Looping a string back over itself to secure it to the post of tuning machine. Numbers 4-6 show methods of dealing with string ends.

Twelve-string guitars

The tuning of a twelve-string guitar is simple. There are six courses of two strings each. The right hand string of each course (most are fatter than the one on the left) is tuned like a six-string guitar: E, A, D, G, B, E. Traditionally the string on the left of the courses E, A, D, G, is tuned one octave above the one on the right side of the course. The strings in the dual courses B and E are tuned to the same note and octave, that is in unison. Because the high G string often breaks, some twelve-string players prefer to tune these strings in unison and not have one an octave higher. If you do this, both G strings should be of the heavier G's gauge.

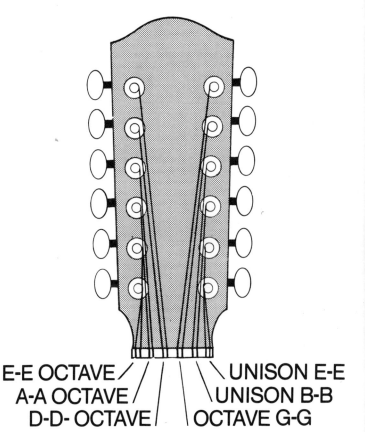

E-E OCTAVE / / / | \ \ UNISON E-E
A-A OCTAVE / / | \ UNISON B-B
D-D- OCTAVE / | \ OCTAVE G-G

FIGURE 20 Tuning of a twelve-string guitar.

Fretted octave matching is particularly effective in tuning twelve-string guitars. See page 17.

Index

Printed in England by
Panda Press, Haverhill, Suffolk.